The Orchard

a parable

Elisa Morgan

Revell
Grand Rapids, Michigan

Published by Fleming H. Revell
a division of Baker Publishing Group
P.O. Box 6287, Grand Rapids, MI 49516-6287

Printed in the United States of America

ISBN 10: 0-8007-1892-5
ISBN 978-0-8007-1892-3

Published in association with the literary agency of Alive
Communications, Inc., 7680 Goddard Street, Suite 200,
Colorado Springs, CO 80920.

Photo credit: Robert Medvedenko pp. 1, 5, 13, 15, 18, 23, 25,
29, 38, 45, 50, 53, 59, 68, 71, 73, 77, 79, 82, 85, 89

To Carol . . .
for modeling what it means
to grow a life that matters.

Most of us want to live productive and meaningful lives—lives that matter. But too often we fall short of this desire. If our lives are like orchards, the fruit is measly, and the land is overrun with weeds and brambles.

The Bible describes this struggle in the book of Galatians. It says we produce two kinds of fruit—

either the good fruit of the Spirit:

love, joy, peace, patience, kindness, goodness, faithfulness, gentleness, and self-control

or the fruitless results of our own sin: HATRED, SELFISHNESS, RAGE, ENVY, BITTERNESS, and the like.

The parable that follows provides an opportunity
to take an inventory of the fruit in your own life.

What is growing—

or not growing—there?

Take a walk in the
orchard of your life,

visit there with the Orchard Keeper,
and learn from his ways.

How vividly
I remember
that Saturday
morning!

I t started like so many others, but its ending was anything but expected.

I'd been to town on errands and was returning home, close to noon. I was ahead of schedule, and so when I came upon the roadside fruit stand, I stopped. Under the canopied cover, bins of fruit wafted their tangy and sweet aroma, inviting me closer. With an ear-to-ear grin, the attendant beckoned me with a brown bag for filling.

"Mornin'! Help yourself. Ya know there's no better fruit in the land."

I nodded. Indeed. I'd often stopped for a load and was never disappointed in my purchase. Crisp, fresh apples. Oranges with skin so spongy it begged for peeling. Pears free of the pockmarked blemishes of the grocery store.

"Ya know, they're all grown right here in The Orchard—right over the hill." The attendant gestured in a vague direction.

I looked off in the distance, and that's when I noticed what I'd never seen before: a simple wooden plank, nailed crossways to a fencepost, that read, "The Orchard." I'd stopped at this fruit stand ump-teen times in the past year and had never noticed the sign.

I was amazed.

"Really? All this fruit is grown right here?" I raised my eyebrows to the attendant. *How could that be?* I asked myself.

"Sure 'nuff. The Orchard Keeper can grow anything. You can go see for yourself if you like." There came that gesture again—off beyond the sign. I followed the attendant's eyes and noticed a faint path threading through the grass.

"Yep, you can hike on up the path and see where this fruit is grown. You can meet the Orchard Keeper for yourself!"

Meeting the Orchard Keeper

W hy not? I set out down the path, looking back once at the attendant and receiving another broad grin and an eager nod for encouragement. The dirt under my feet rose as I climbed a rather steep hill. The path crested, and a sight I'll never forget stalled me in my tracks.

Stretched out over the countryside for miles were trees laden with apples, oranges, pears, peaches . . . and some other varieties I couldn't make out—were those bananas? What an unlikely combination! Impossible! I stuffed my hands in my pockets and took in the view. I'd never imagined what lay over this hill.

Just then a figure appeared from a clearing between trees. Dressed in jeans and a work shirt, he wore tan leather gloves, but his head was bare to the sun. He carried a set of simple tools: rake, hoe, and trowel. A bolt of twine stuck out of the back pocket of his jeans. He looked up and met my gaze, his eyes both welcoming and challenging at once. His mouth broke into that same open grin I'd seen in the attendant back at the fruit stand.

"Hello! Welcome to The Orchard." His arms swept wide about him. "What brought you here?"

A simple question. Why had I come?

"I guess to see where the fruit came from," I stammered. "I've stopped here for years to buy fruit and never before noticed the sign and, well, do you really grow this incredible fruit—all of it—right here?"

"Yes, I do."

"All in one orchard? How is that possible? I could never do that!" My mind swirled at the thought of all the sweat, smarts, and money it would take to grow multiple fruit in one orchard.

"No, I don't imagine you could. But with me, everything is possible. I'm the Orchard Keeper."

I didn't know what to say to that. His words sounded gran-
diose—almost arrogant. But when I met his eyes, there was a
humility I'd rarely encountered. He wasn't bragging. He was
just telling the truth.

I was even more interested.

The Orchard Keeper turned toward the trees and beckoned me to follow. "See, I mapped this orchard out specifically to contain a variety of fruit. A wide selection is important because folks don't like the same kind of fruit. Some prefer citrus, others stone fruit, and still others the classic apple or pear. I plant all types of fruit to meet the appetites of all types of people. And I also make sure my fruit is the best it can be—from the skin to the seed. The best fruit. All varieties of fruit. That's what brought you here, isn't it—the fruit?" I thought about his question and realized indeed, it was the fruit that had beckoned me to stop my car, to notice the sign,

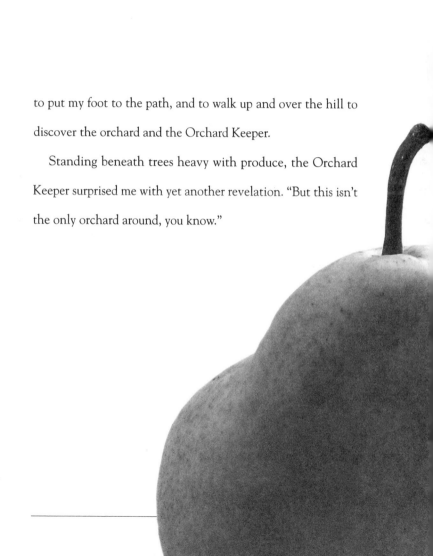

to put my foot to the path, and to walk up and over the hill to discover the orchard and the Orchard Keeper.

Standing beneath trees heavy with produce, the Orchard Keeper surprised me with yet another revelation. "But this isn't the only orchard around, you know."

An Unlikely Orchard

Surprise swept over me again . . . I'd lived in the area for years. What was he saying? I couldn't think of a single orchard between here and my own house.

"Where?"

"Well, right in your own neighborhood—in fact, your own land was intended as an orchard."

Mentally, I inventoried the meager offerings of my yard. There were those two scraggly pear trees on the left side of my lot. A stand of scrawny cherries. A few apples that still produced. Oh—and I'd staked up a potted lemon bush I'd carried back from vacation in Florida. I was rather proud of that little lemon—as I'd actually coaxed a fruit or two from its branches. But an orchard? Hardly.

The Orchard Keeper went on as if I'd been speaking out loud. "Well, with the right care, those pear trees can produce. Same with the cherries. And the apples are already quite productive. With some pruning, care, and a few lessons taken to heart, your trees will produce fruit beyond your imagination."

"And the lemon?"

I couldn't resist.

"Well now, we'll have to talk about that lemon," he smiled. "Want to take a look? Want me to come with you and show you what I can do with your orchard?"

For a moment I wavered. I thought of the weeds. The gangly branches of trees I'd left untended. I'd had many good intentions, but other things had taken over my attention. And then I wondered what I really had to lose. The land seemed beyond my help. Why not? This had become a day of why nots. With the Orchard Keeper at my side, I made my way back down the path, past the grinning gaze of the attendant, and got into my car. "You sure you have time for this?" I asked as I started the engine.

"It's what I do," the Orchard Keeper replied as he settled in next to me.

Land

Management

The trip was short. As we pulled into my drive, I cringed at the disarray. Gathering my best outlook, I braced myself for a quick tour. The Orchard Keeper followed me about my property, surveying my holdings. When we returned to our starting place, he faced me with a question. "Okay. You brought me here to your property. For years, you've done what you wanted with it, and now you have this to show for it. Are you satisfied with what you've accomplished? Is this what you want from your land?"

The question was direct. Part of me wanted time to think about my response. Lots of time. Of course I wasn't satisfied with what I'd accomplished! What did he think? But there was only so much time and energy and money to invest. I'd grown accustomed to the messy result.

I looked over my land again, this time with new eyes. There were weeds everywhere. Out-of-control weeds. And suckers coming up from the roots of the trees in odd spots. The branches of the trees seemed schizophrenic, spouting shoots in all directions. Rotten fruit and damaged branches lay on the ground like a dumped load someone just couldn't carry another step. But there, on my front porch, sheltered by the awning, my little lemon tree huddled, clutching a single yellow fruit in its skinny arms. Perhaps my trees lacked flair, even begged for mercy, but the lemon was bearing. Not all bad.

Still, I knew where the Orchard Keeper was headed with his question. No, this wasn't what I wanted for my land. Surely he had something better in mind. Why not?

Once again, he read my thoughts.

"So you want more?
You want to see
what I can grow here?"
I nodded.

"Then you'll have to give me control. You must yield to me and allow me to be the Orchard Keeper that I am. Okay?"

I nodded again, even though I wasn't sure what all was involved in "yielding." Soon, I would find out.

The
Pruning Process

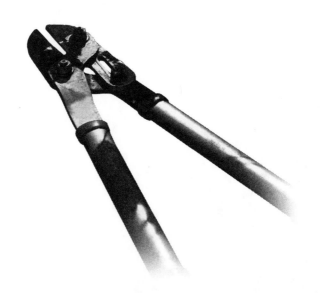

L et's get started."

He headed first toward the pears. "Ah, these sweet trees," he said fondly. "But they're so much smaller than I imagined. Do they produce any fruit at all?"

"Not in the past few years," I murmured. I remembered my grandmother boiling piles of pears into jellies and jams, canning them for Christmas gifts, and sharing them fresh with neighbors. But to be honest, I wasn't sure what to do with the pears. I hadn't paid much attention to my grandmother's work. I wouldn't know where to begin.

"They'll need a good pruning," the Orchard Keeper pronounced. I hadn't noticed the shears he'd been carrying, but now he pulled them out and set to work. "Could you get me a ladder from the garage?" he asked over his shoulder. When I returned, ladder in tow, he'd clambered up the tree trunk and was sending down bough after bough of diseased wood to the ground. The tree suddenly looked off balance, as if bitten by a hungry wind, leaving unsightly gashes in its foliage. I didn't like it.

"Don't take
so much off!"
I objected.
"You're making it
ugly!"

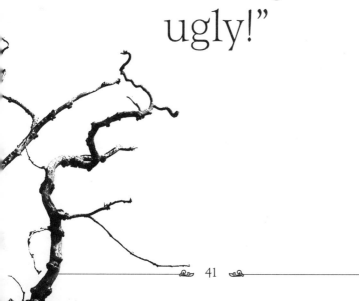

The Orchard Keeper paused midcut and looked at me. "Every gardener knows you hard prune the weak shoots and light prune the stronger growth. If you want healthy fruit and lots of it—I have to prune. If this tree had been properly shaped and trained when it was young, and kept that way, I wouldn't have to prune so much now. But there's so much damage . . . if fruit were to try to grow from these branches, they would break from the weight. Pruning will strengthen these branches to bear the kind of harvest I've had in mind. Just wait . . . come spring it'll be worth it."

I took a step back and watched, sliding my hands into my pockets to keep them from interfering.

The Orchard Keeper finished one pear tree and then moved on to the second, leaving them both looking scalped.

I shuddered.

What had I done, inviting him here?

What would he do next?

Deep Root
Feeding

I didn't have to wait long to find out. Sheathing his shears like a sword, he grabbed the ladder and headed for the cherries. There was a small stand of them, seven in all. Their leaves, small, mottled, and shriveled, rattled in the breeze. His eye went straight to the soil.

Dry.

He bent down and took a handful of dirt in his hands, rubbing it between his fingers as it spilled back to the ground like sand through an hourglass.

"Get me a pitchfork—will you? And a hose."

When I returned with the requested items, he thanked me and began poking holes in the caked ground while softening it with water from the garden hose. "This needs to soak, so I'll leave the water running while we go to the next area."

Wall Repair

Once again he rose to his feet, eyed his surroundings, and headed off, toward the rock wall that protected my land from the wild. Originally, the wall was constructed to keep out deer, raccoons, and coyotes—all the unwanted invaders that would strip my land of its produce. But with the lack of attention to my fruit trees and their lack of production came a corresponding lack of concern for the wall and its eventual disrepair. What did it matter if the animals trespassed if there was so little fruit for them to steal?

Erosion had become familiar to me. Apathy replaced my once-zealous passion for my property and its potential.

Just then the Orchard Keeper approached the wall,
                    and suddenly I remembered. . . .

"Why is this storage shed here against the wall?" he asked. "It's so far away from the trees, how can it possibly be helpful? What do you keep in here, anyway?" His hand was on the latch handle before I could stop him.

Once open,

the door revealed the truth:

Nothing.

There was nothing inside.

Only space leading to a larger opening, this one in the wall itself. See, the wall had begun to crumble, and for a while, I'd diligently worked to shore it up. But one day it seemed like just too much effort, there were other things to do . . . and I had an idea. I decided to cover up the hole with a makeshift toolshed—a facade. The toolshed would look efficient and respectable. No one needed to know it was just covering up the hole in the wall around my land—the hole I'd given up repairing.

But I knew that the toolshed hadn't solved the problem. Later I discovered deer and even coyotes on my property. I wasn't really surprised to see them there, and I traced their tracks back to a growing gap in the wall behind the shed. All my efforts to repair that gap exhausted me. I'd invested time, money, and energy wheeling load after load of cement to shore it up, but my hastily fixed patches always crumbled during the next rain or temperature change. I was fed up with the ever-widening gap.

Too much. Too big. Too late. While I'd grown accustomed to its presence in my life, before the Orchard Keeper I felt ashamed, and then beneath that, a profound sense of loss. I knew I'd settled. I'd given up on the very discipline required to ensure safety and security and hope and health for the rest of my property. As a landowner, entrusted with providing for the land under my care, I had failed. Further, I felt I *was* a failure.

The Orchard Keeper met my gaze. Instead of responding with judgment, disgust, or rejection, he gently offered, "I can fix this for you, if you want me to."

I bowed my head, looked at the ground, and nodded.

Relief filled my heart.

Within minutes, the shed was gone. He gathered the dismantled pieces into a neat pile, added the pruned pear branches, and set the stack ablaze. Next he launched himself through the wall's hole into the wild and returned with enough rocks to repair the hole. Once he had set them in place, he smoothed cement in the cracks and then, wiping his hands, smiled at me with confidence.

"*Remember this:* there is no hole too big or too much for me to fix, and it is never too late to repair what has been ruined.

Now, let's get back to those cherries."

Rooted Growth

After the water soaking, the ground was now soft. "Sometimes the ground is too dry to receive the food a tree needs. Then the roots end up at the surface like these. We need to remind these roots which direction to grow: down, toward the water every day. Then they'll be able to transport the food required by the rest of the tree."

*"Ah . . . now a deep root
feeding will net results
in the coming seasons."*

The
Compost Pile

Say, if it's a lush cherry crop we're after, we'll need more than food at the roots. Let's add a layer of food near the surface. Compost. Got any?"

What an understatement! In the far corner of my lot stood an enormous bin, overflowing with refuse. There had been many days when I'd cynically concluded that the only thing growing on my entire property was that pile of garbage scraps.

The Orchard Keeper surmised my conclusion and then responded, "It does seem a large pile of debris. Failures. Unfinished efforts. Such unwanted items, such discards from your days, can become the fertilizer for fruitful production. Fruit production

requires compost. In fact, the best fruit grows from layers of it. Come. Let's scoop up a few loads and lavish those cherries with promise!"

I'd never really considered the positive side of compost. I'd always seen it as refuse. But with the perspective provided by the Orchard Keeper, what I'd defined as waste became purposeful. I grabbed two shovels, and in no time, we'd hauled several heaps from the compost pile to the cherry trees, layering the rich, though stinky, soil about their trunks. Once accomplished, we stepped back and together evaluated our work. Yes. In time, the cherries would show the results of our investment.

Container
Garden

I'd begun to recover from the wall fiasco. I knew the Orchard Keeper meant what he said about fixing the holes in my wall—both present and future. I felt hopeful and renewed. And then at the cherry trees, I felt comfortable and confident taking in his direction for growth in the seasons ahead. Time for a break, I decided, and I invited him to my house for some refreshment.

As we approached my front door, the Orchard Keeper noticed my lemon tree. "Ah . . . so this is the lemon you spoke of?" I nodded proudly. Maybe it was a little scrawny and weak, but it was growing a real fruit. I wasn't a total failure after all! TA DA!

"I notice that you have kept this tree quite close to your house. You've sheltered it with the awning over the porch. You've staked it up in its pot here. I even see a hose curled up next to it and a spritzer bottle for keeping it moist."

"Yes!" I responded eagerly. "Aren't I doing a great job with it?"

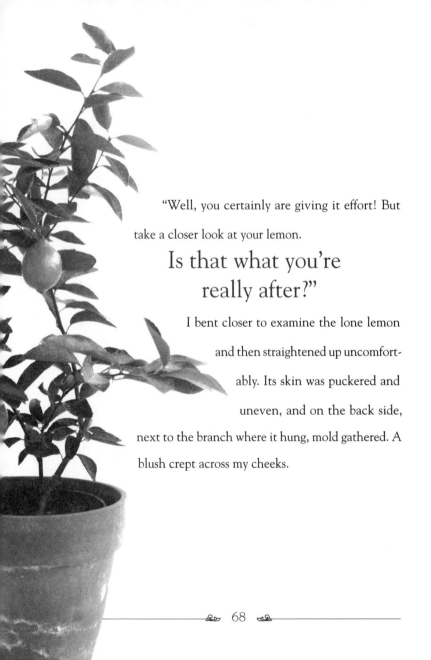

"Well, you certainly are giving it effort! But take a closer look at your lemon.

Is that what you're really after?"

I bent closer to examine the lone lemon and then straightened up uncomfortably. Its skin was puckered and uneven, and on the back side, next to the branch where it hung, mold gathered. A blush crept across my cheeks.

"The fact is that I never grew that fruit. This fruit is of your own design and effort. At first glance, it's attractive and winsome, but when you get closer, you catch the flaws. All your efforts have been invested here, in this immigrated fruit, rather than in the fruit I designed for your days. Besides that, it's clear that you intend to keep this fruit in its container. You have no intention of planting it permanently on the land I gave you. This fruit is adequate, but it's not mine."

Suddenly the lemon looked rotten to me. I had no desire for it. I realized I'd grown it out of my desire to control something for myself. I brought it from another land and plunked it down in a container on the porch, pouring my total gardening efforts into it and ignoring the larger fruit production under my nose. I thought it made me look good, but instead, I could see the effort was futile.

After a brief rest on the porch and lemonade made from a can rather than the moldy lemon, the Orchard Keeper raised his eyes to the apple trees. They were next.

Good Apples

I thought the apples wouldn't be so bad since they were still producing fruit. I was wrong. That was the problem. They were indeed producing fruit. And it was all rotting on the ground.

The Orchard Keeper wasn't exactly angry, but there was no mistaking his disappointment as he approached the apple trees and their discarded fruit below. Squirrels fled as he drew near, grabbing what they could and scampering up trunks and into bushes. Mounds of apples remained in their wake, though none fit for human consumption. Instead, burgundy skin broke, oozing yellowed, mushy pulp underfoot as we surrounded the stand.

"What a waste."

His words were factual. Truthful. Again, there was no judgment. Just the honest truth and its accompanying grief. In hearing his unembellished words, I knew he was right.

Why had I let all those apples go to waste?

I thought back to the unpruned pears. I'd disdained the "ugly" task necessary to strengthen their branches to bear fruit. With the unfed cherries, I'd ignored the deep application of water and the need for stinky fertilizer that would improve their crop. The lemon had been about control—my control over what grew and didn't grow in my life. The unrepaired wall grew more and more damaged from my inability to fight the forces of nature. Too much. Too big. I'd given up . . . until the Orchard Keeper had encouraged me to invite *his* efforts into the fix. He could mend what I could not. I remembered the relief of surrendering to his work. Pruning. Feeding. Yielding. Protecting. All were part of his plan to grow fruit in my orchard.

The wasted apples? It wasn't that fruit *wouldn't* grow in my orchard. Apples grew despite my lack of attention. The issue of the apples was that I was intimidated by their presence. They were so bountiful. I'd done so little—nothing to aid their growth. I didn't deserve such fruit. Nor so much of it. How could I ever use it wisely?

Just a few feet off, the Orchard Keeper smiled at my process-ing, nodded at my conclusion. "Yes. You don't have to be good enough to grow fruit. My job is to produce fruit. Your job is to cooperate with me as I grow fruit and to make room for it in your days. It's not about you. And it's not all up to you. I meant the harvest to be yours to enjoy and to use, not to worry and fret over or to weigh you down."

Offering yet another invitation, he continued, "Now, let's gather up what's left on these branches and box it up for your own fruit stand. What do you say?"

I hurried to the garage where fruit boxes had been stored but never used and returned to the Orchard Keeper. Together, we pulled apples from branches and nestled them in the waiting boxes until we had packed almost five full to the brim. I climbed down from the ladder and surveyed the stack of produce. Not bad. Not bad at all.

"No, in fact, very good!"
the Orchard Keeper
pronounced.

A Walk
in the Orchard

I f you like, I will stay here with you and continue the work of fruit production." I have some ideas for some new varieties we could bring in over where the shed used to be. By this time next year, you ought to have many varieties of fruit for your own fruit stand down the lane. Folks like all kinds of fruit, you know. Between now and then, though, will you make a pact with me?"

My trust in the Orchard Keeper was growing. I swallowed the lump rising in my throat and questioned, "A pact? What kind?"

"Just stroll with me. Every day, join me in the orchard here. Together we can take an inventory of areas that are growing well and areas that need attention and dream of new areas to begin growing. I like being with you. I want to hear your ideas. And remember, you don't have to grow fruit on your own. Your job is to welcome me into your land to do my work. My job is fruit production."

I looked full into the Orchard Keeper's face, free in my response.

"You bet. Produce your fruit in my land. All of your fruit in all of my land.

After all, folks like all kinds of fruit, you know."

Fruit Markets

I t was a Saturday like so many before and so many since. A car pulled up at my fruit stand, and the driver emerged, eyes glued to the pears, apples, cherries and, yes, even lemons in the bins about me.

"What beautiful fruit! Where does it come from?" the driver asked. I smiled and gestured at the sign to my side that read, "The Orchard." The driver's gaze followed my eyes to the path next to the sign. "I'd like to see where this path leads. Mind if I explore?" came the next question.

I smiled, bowed, and murmured, "Why not? Hike on up the path and see for yourself where this fruit is grown."

Go and meet
the Orchard
Keeper!

"So I say,

live by the Spirit,

and you will not gratify the desires of the sinful nature.
For the sinful nature desires what is contrary to the Spirit,
and the Spirit what is contrary to the sinful nature.
They are in conflict with each other, so that you do not do
what you want. But if you are

led by the Spirit,

you are not under law."

"But the fruit of the Spirit is

love, joy, peace, patience, kindness, goodness, faithfulness, gentleness, and self-control.

Against such things there is no law."

Galatians 5:16-18, 22-23

The story you've just read is a parable—an earthly story with a heavenly meaning. There is no literal Orchard nor is there a literal Orchard Keeper. However, the lush fruit of character that grows from a life well-lived—as described in this story—does exist. It grows in the lives of those who know God through his Son, Jesus Christ.

Do you know Jesus? The Bible tells us, "For God so loved the world that he gave his one and only Son, that whoever believes in him shall not perish but have eternal life" (John 3:16).

Knowing Jesus is simple. Just stop and pray a prayer something like this: *Dear Jesus, I want to know you. I need your help. I believe you died on the cross for my sins—my mistakes and faults and shortcomings. Please forgive me. Please come into my life and begin a relationship with me. Amen.*

Knowing Jesus means that you become a follower of Christ . . . seeking after who he is and what he says in all aspects of your life. When Jesus prayed for his disciples on the last night of his life on earth, he said, "I chose you and appointed you to go and bear fruit—fruit that will last" (John 15:16). Knowing Jesus means growing the fruit of his spirit in ourselves. That fruit is evidence of our spiritual growth. And as it becomes visible in our day-to-day existence, it attracts others to Jesus and to the hope they can have through relationship with him.

Are you ready to grow a life that matters?

Elisa Morgan is president and CEO of MOPS International, Inc. (www.mops.org), based in Denver, Colorado. She is the author of *Naked Fruit* (the book that inspired the parable of *The Orchard*) and *Twinkle*, as well as the author or editor of nine other books. Elisa lives with her family in Centennial, Colorado.